THE
LAST JEDI

Written by Beth Davies

Editor Beth Davies
Designer Chris Gould
Pre-production Producer Marc Staples
Producer Louise Daly
Managing Editor Paula Regan
Managing Art Editor Jo Connor
Publisher Julie Ferris
Art Director Lisa Lanzarini
Publishing Director Simon Beecroft

First American Edition, 2018
Published in the United States by DK Publishing
345 Hudson Street, New York, New York 10014

Page design copyright © 2018 Dorling Kindersley Limited
DK, a Division of Penguin Random House LLC
18 19 20 21 22 10 9 8 7 6 5 4 3 2 1
001–307152–March/2018

ISBN 978-1-4654-6663-1 (Paperback)
ISBN 978-1-4654-6664-8 (Library edition)

A WORLD OF IDEAS:
SEE ALL THERE IS TO KNOW

www.dk.com
www.LEGO.com/starwars
www.starwars.com

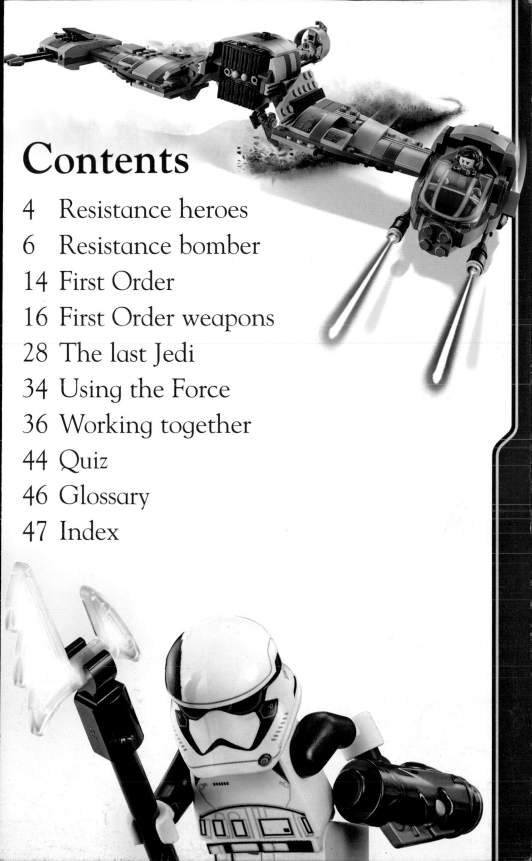

Contents

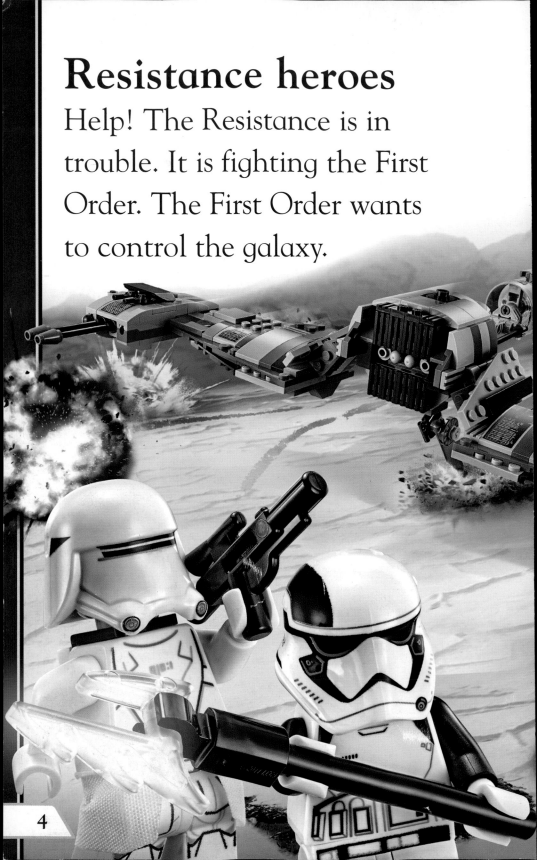

Resistance heroes

Help! The Resistance is in trouble. It is fighting the First Order. The First Order wants to control the galaxy.

The Resistance must stop them.
The Resistance heroes are a small
group but they are very brave.

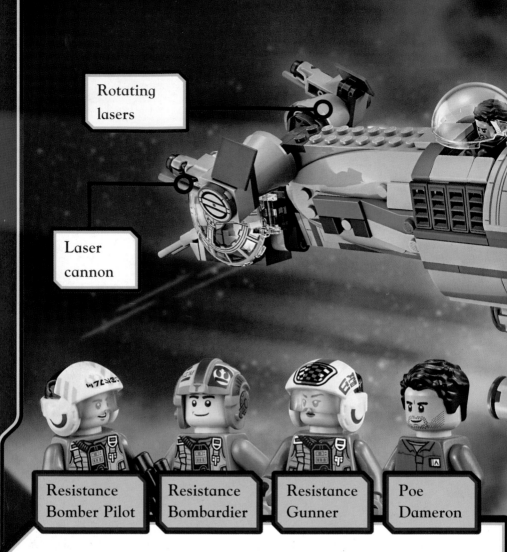

Rotating lasers

Laser cannon

Resistance Bomber Pilot

Resistance Bombardier

Resistance Gunner

Poe Dameron

Resistance bomber

The Resistance has a tiny fleet of spaceships. Small Resistance crews must work hard to defeat the First Order and its huge craft.

Communication antenna

Main cockpit

Weapons storage area

Ball gunner turret

Targeting system

General Leia Organa is the leader of the Resistance. She has fought in many battles during her life.

Vice Admiral Holdo   Admiral Ackbar   General Ematt

Vice Admiral Holdo is a friend of General Leia. She takes control of the Resistance when Leia is injured.

Admiral Ackbar commands the biggest ship in the Resistance. General Ematt commands troops on the ground.

Holdo and Poe often disagree with each other.

Poe Dameron is one of the bravest pilots in the Resistance. He is not very good at following orders. He often gets into trouble.

Poe respects General Leia but does not trust Vice Admiral Holdo. He has his own plan to save the Resistance.

Finn used to be part of the First Order. Now he is a Resistance fighter. Finn was badly hurt in battle. He is upset because he has been separated from his friend, Rey.

Finn is given a special mission. He hopes he can help the Resistance and stop the fighting.

First Order

Look out! The First Order is
chasing the Resistance. It has many
ships in its fleet, including 30 huge
Star Destroyers.

Every First Order ship is filled
with soldiers and weapons.
They can conquer entire planets.
The Resistance must be quick!

First Order weapons

The First Order takes control of planets with the help of tough vehicles and equipment. The First Order is a very dangerous group!

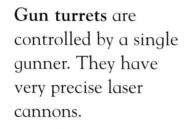

Gun turrets are controlled by a single gunner. They have very precise laser cannons.

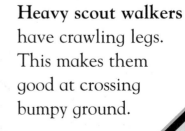

Heavy scout walkers have crawling legs. This makes them good at crossing bumpy ground.

6

Star Destroyers have large crews and lots of weapons. They often serve as a base for senior First Order officers.

Heavy assault walkers tower over enemies on the ground. These huge walkers have space inside for transporting troops.

First Order Stormtrooper   First Order Executioner

The First Order has an army
of highly skilled soldiers. These
soldiers are called stormtroopers.
They fight battles against the

First Order Walker Driver   First Order Flametrooper

Stormtroopers have strong
armor and carry powerful weapons.
Stormtroopers can be trained
to do special jobs or to work in
different places.

There are also lots of officers
working for the First Order.
It is their job to carry out the
First Order's plans.

The officers work on ships and
in First Order bases, so they do
not need armor.

Droids help the officers carry out their tasks.

BB-9E
is a First
Order droid.

General Hux is a young officer.
He is very important. He commands
all of the First Order officers. He
wants to destroy the Resistance.

Captain Phasma leads the stormtroopers. She is very skilled in battle. She expects everyone to follow her orders.

First Order staff fear Supreme Leader Snoke.

Supreme Leader Snoke is the leader of the First Order. He gives orders to General Hux. His base is a huge Mega-Destroyer starship.

Snoke is skilled in the dark side of the Force. The Force is a powerful energy. Snoke uses the Force to try to control the galaxy.

Snoke has an apprentice named Kylo Ren. Kylo is General Leia's son but Kylo does not speak to his family.

Kylo Ren is strong in the dark side of the Force. Snoke believes Kylo can help him defeat the Resistance. Kylo secretly wants Snoke's power for himself.

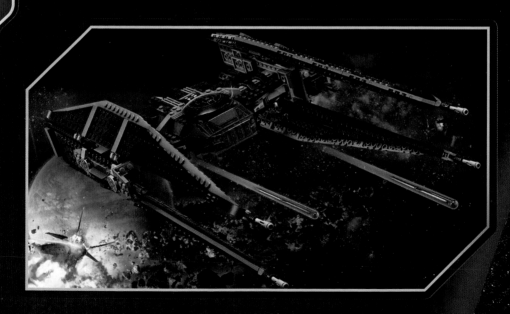

Kylo Ren flies a TIE silencer starfighter.

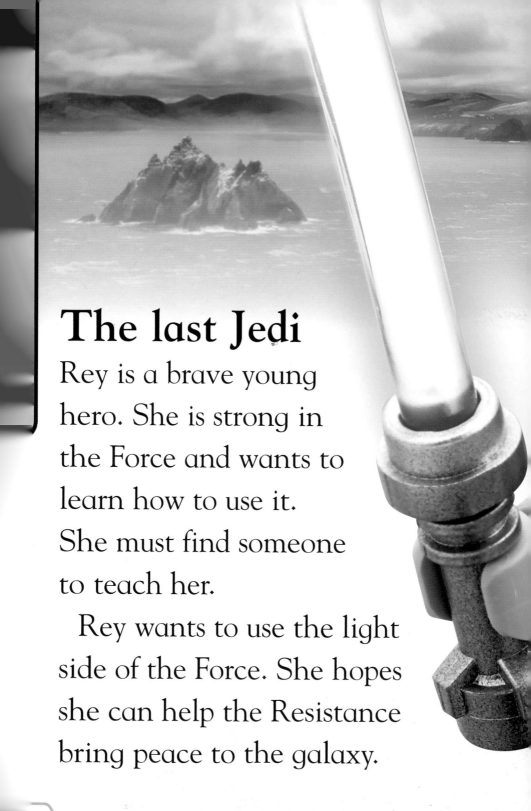

The last Jedi

Rey is a brave young
hero. She is strong in
the Force and wants to
learn how to use it.
She must find someone
to teach her.

Rey wants to use the light
side of the Force. She hopes
she can help the Resistance
bring peace to the galaxy.

The Jedi were a group of beings who protected the galaxy many years ago. They have all been destroyed, except for one.

Rey must find the last Jedi and ask for his help. The last Jedi is named Luke Skywalker. He is General Leia's brother.

Luke does not want to use the Force anymore. He lives alone on a planet called Ahch-To. He is the only human, but there are also friendly birds called porgs.

R2-D2 and Chewbacca go
with Rey to find Luke. They
are old friends of Luke's.
They want Luke to
help Rey.

Using the Force

Rey and Kylo Ren are both strong in the Force. The powers that they learn are very different, though.

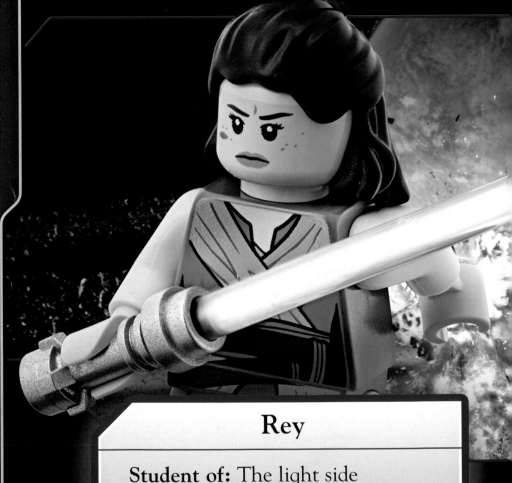

Rey

Student of: The light side
Special skills: Flying starships and hand-to-hand combat
Parents: Unknown
Mentor: Luke Skywalker

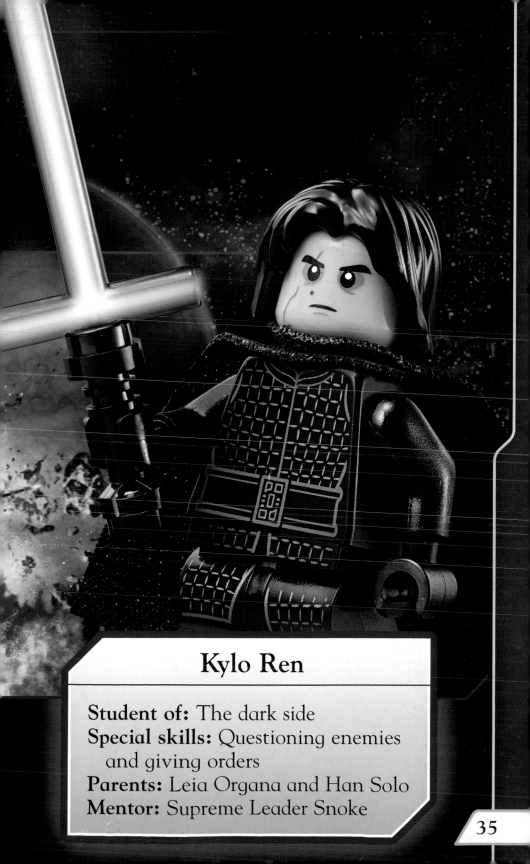

Kylo Ren

Student of: The dark side
Special skills: Questioning enemies
and giving orders
Parents: Leia Organa and Han Solo
Mentor: Supreme Leader Snoke

Working together

Rose Tico works as a technician for the Resistance. She repairs starfighters when they are damaged in battle. She wants to defeat the First Order more than anything.

Rose has an older sister named Paige. Paige is a gunner on a Resistance ship. Both sisters are very brave.

Rose and Finn must work together on a mission for the Resistance. They hide away on a shuttle.

The shuttle is so small the First Order will not notice them. Good luck, Rose and Finn!

BB-8 has joined Rose and Finn on their mission! BB-8 is a loyal droid. He has many talents.

The team must find a codebreaker who can help them break into Snoke's Mega-Destroyer. They must be careful not to get caught.

The Resistance heroes must all try
their best if they want to stop Snoke
and Kylo Ren. Poe must protect the
Resistance fleet from harm.

Finn and Rose must find a way
onto Snoke's Mega-Destroyer. Rey
must learn to use the Force. Together,
they can defeat the First Order.

Quiz

1. Who is General Leia's son?

2. What planet does Luke Skywalker live on?

3. Who travels with Rey to find Luke?

4. What is Rose's job?

5. Who leads the First Order stormtroopers?

6. How many Star Destroyers does the First Order have?

7. Who takes control of the Resistance when Leia is injured?

8. Which droid joins Finn and Rose on their mission?

9. True or false? Supreme Leader Snoke is strong in the light side of the Force.

10. What are porgs?

Answers on page 47.

Glossary

apprentice
Someone who is studying
with a teacher.

command
The action of giving an order or leading.

conquer
To take control of a place or group using an army.

droid
A robot or machine that does a specific job.

First Order
A group that seeks to rule the galaxy.

mentor
Someone who trains or guides someone else.

Resistance
A group that defends the galaxy from the
First Order.

technician
A person whose job it is to maintain equipment.

troop
A group of soldiers working together.

Index

Answers to the quiz on pages 44 and 45:
1. Kylo Ren 2. Ahch-To 3. R2-D2 and Chewbacca 4. Technician
5. Captain Phasma 6. 30 7. Vice Admiral Holdo 8. BB-8 9. False—
Snoke is strong in the dark side 10. Friendly birds

A LEVEL FOR EVERY READER

This book is a part of an exciting four-level reading series to support children in developing the habit of reading widely for both pleasure and information. Each book is designed to develop a child's reading skills, fluency, grammar awareness, and comprehension in order to build confidence and enjoyment when reading.

Ready for a Level 2 (Beginning to Read) book

A child should:

- be able to recognize a bank of common words quickly and be able to blend sounds together to make some words.
- be familiar with using beginner letter sounds and context clues to figure out unfamiliar words.
- sometimes correct his/her reading if it doesn't look right or make sense.
- be aware of the need for a slight pause at commas and a longer one at periods.

A valuable and shared reading experience

For many children, reading requires much effort, but adult participation can make reading both fun and easier. Here are a few tips on how to use this book with a young reader:

Check out the contents together:

- read about the book on the back cover and talk about the contents page to help heighten interest and expectation.
- discuss new or difficult words.
- chat about labels, annotations, and pictures.

Support the reader:

- give the book to the young reader to turn the pages.
- where necessary, encourage longer words to be broken into syllables, sound out each one, and then flow the syllables together; ask him/her to reread the sentence to check the meaning.
- encourage the reader to vary her/his voice as she/he reads; demonstrate how to do this if helpful.

Talk at the end of each book, or after every few pages:

- ask questions about the text and the meaning of the words used—this helps develop comprehension skills.
- read the quiz at the end of the book and encourage the reader to answer the questions, if necessary, by turning back to the relevant pages to find the answers.

31901062727427